# A PRACTICAL GUIDE TO

# Herbs & Spices

# A PRACTICAL GUIDE TO

# Herbs & Spices

## Exciting recipes for creative cooking

### EDITED BY KATE CRANSHAW

COOMBE BOOKS

# Introduction

It's hard to imagine cooking without herbs and spices. So accustomed are we to the richness of flavour, vibrancy of colour and the delicacy of aroma that the food we eat would be sadly lacking without these vital ingredients.

Supermarkets are now well stocked with a huge array of ground and whole spices, dried, frozen and fresh cut herbs and even 'live' herbs growing in compost. The choice is almost overwhelming but the potential for creating delicious recipes at home has never been better.

Today's enthusiasm for trying food and flavours from different countries lies behind much of the growth in the availability of herbs and spices. But these ingredients are by no means new. Herbs have a long tradition of use in British homes that dates back centuries and encompasses both cooking and healing roles. Today there is also a revival of interest in the healing power of herbs, and herb teas are once more becoming popular for their refreshing quality as well as their mild therapeutic properties. Try camomile to ease insomnia or mint to aid digestion.

The role of herbs in cooking has never been in question however. Essential oils present in the leaves, stems and flowers of the plant are released on cutting, chopping or crushing. It is therefore important to use fresh herbs as soon as possible after chopping for maximum flavour. Any extra can be stored in the fridge, wrapped in a little damp kitchen paper in a plastic bag. Alternatively, larger amounts, such as parsley, can be placed in a jug of water out of the direct sun. Dried herbs are a convenient and cheaper substitute for fresh. Store in airtight jars, ideally in a cupboard away from the light. Remember when using dried herbs that their flavour has been concentrated, so use 1tsp (5ml) to 1tbsp (15ml) of fresh herbs in recipes.

Recipes often suggest adding fresh herbs just before the end of cooking for a lovely vibrancy of flavour and colour. In contrast, spices tend to be associated with long, slow cooking to enrich and give a distinctive depth of flavour and colour to food. Spices are widely used in traditional British cakes, pastries, bread and biscuits but as a nation we are now becoming far more adventurous with their use in savoury recipes.

The traditional dishes of Asia feature large quantities of cinnamon, cloves, ginger and pepper, all native plants to the region. As trade and transport improved over the centuries these ingredients found their way into European kitchens, being ideally suited to travel as they are dried for storage.

Obviously, as spices are the dried aromatic parts of plants, they come in all manner of shapes and colours. This includes bark, seeds, pods, stalks and berries. Bought whole, they may be used intact in recipes, sometimes being removed before eating – cardamom pods, cloves and cinnamon sticks for example are not recommended for eating! More usually spices are ground before cooking. Keen cooks may choose to do this themselves using either the traditional pestle and mortar or a small electric coffee grinder, reserved for this purpose. Alternatively, buy ready ground spices, storing them in airtight containers, in a cupboard away from the light. Different spices are often used together to give wonderful flavours characteristic of certain styles of cuisine. Chinese five spice powder for example, widely used in oriental cooking is a blend of ground cloves, cassia, fennel seeds, star anise and anise pepper to give a powerful anise flavour.

The scope for introducing exciting new flavours and for rediscovering more familiar tastes is almost limitless. Let herbs and spices add a whole new dimension to your cooking.

# Pea Soup with Mint

Preparation takes about 30 minutes, cooking takes 45-50 minutes.

Serves 8-10

Other fresh herbs, such as marjoram, chervil or thyme may be substituted for the mint.

## INGREDIENTS

175g/6oz dried split peas
570g/1¼lbs frozen peas
90g/3oz fresh mint leaves
120g/4oz butter
Salt and pepper

## METHOD

**1** Place the split peas with about 1.7 ltrs/3pts water in a heavy saucepan. Cover, bring to the boil and cook for about 40 minutes or until very tender. Strain the peas and reserve the liquid.

**2** Pour the liquid back into the saucepan and add the frozen peas. Chop the mint leaves, reserving some whole leaves for garnish, and add to the peas. Bring to the boil in a covered saucepan. Simmer for 5 minutes.

**3** Meanwhile, melt the butter and add to the dried peas. Work in a food processor to form a smooth purée. Add to the green peas, mixing well. Add salt and pepper to taste.

**4** Pour the hot soup into a tureen and garnish with the reserved sprigs or leaves of mint. Serve immediately.

Step 1. Cook the split peas in water until very soft. Test by mashing some against the side of the pan.

Step 3. Purée the split peas and stir them back into the soup, mixing well.

# *Indian Tomato Soup*

## INGREDIENTS

*225g/8oz tomatoes*
*1 medium onion*
*1 green chilli*
*3 cloves garlic*
*2 tbsps vegetable oil*
*1 tbsp tomato purée*
*1 ltr/1¾ pts water, or*
*vegetable stock*
*4-6 green curry leaves*
*Salt*
***Garnish:***
*Coriander leaves*
*Halved chillies*

## METHOD

**1** Cut a small cross in the skin of each tomato and plunge them into boiling water for 30-40 seconds. Remove the tomatoes and carefully peel away the loosened skin with a sharp knife.

**2** Remove the green core from the tomatoes and roughly chop the flesh.

**3** Peel the onion and chop it into small pieces using a sharp knife. Deseed and finely chop the chilli and crush the garlic. Heat the oil in a large saucepan and gently sauté the onion, chilli and garlic for 3-4 minutes until soft, but not browned.

**4** Stir in the chopped tomatoes and cook for 5 minutes, stirring often to prevent the vegetables from burning.

**5** Blend the tomato purée with the water or stock and pour this into the onions and tomatoes. Add the curry leaves, season with the salt and simmer for 5-7 minutes.

**6** Remove the soup from the heat and stir in the coriander leaves and the chilli halves.

**7** Pour the soup into 4-6 serving bowls and serve piping hot, discarding the chilli garnish before eating.

Step 2. Cut away and discard the hard green core from the tomatoes, and chop the flesh roughly with a sharp knife.

Preparation takes about 15 minutes, cooking takes 17-18 minutes.

Serves 4

Great care must be taken when preparing fresh chillies. Try not to get the juice into your eyes or mouth. If this should happen, rinse with lots of cold water.

# Herb Ravioli with Chicken Stock

Preparation takes about 45 minutes and cooking takes about 10 minutes.

Serves 4

The herbs should be visible through the pasta. Pass the sandwiched strips of dough through closely-set rollers on the pasta machine.

Step 3. Cover half the pasta with the leaves.

## INGREDIENTS

*175g/6oz strong plain flour*
*1 large egg, beaten*
*1 bunch chervil*
*1 bunch flat leaf parsley*
*1ltr/1¾ pts chicken stock*
*1 tsp dried rosemary*
*Salt and pepper*

## METHOD

**1** Sift the flour into a mixing bowl with a pinch of salt. Make a well in the centre and add the egg. Mix with the finger tips, gradually incorporating the flour, until a dough is formed. Turn the dough out onto a lightly floured surface and knead for 5-10 minutes or until it is smooth and elastic. Cover and leave to rest for 30 minutes.

**2** Pass the dough through a pasta machine, flouring both sides of the dough as it goes through the rollers to prevent sticking. Continue rolling, increasing the setting number, until the pasta is very thin. Cut the dough into long strips. Alternatively, roll the dough out with a rolling pin until thin enough to see through, and cut into strips.

**3** Spread out half of the strips onto your work surface and cover with the chervil and parsley leaves.

**4** Place the remaining strips on top, press down well along the strips with your fingers and then once again run the strips through the rollers of the pasta machine, or roll with a rolling pin.

**5** Heat the stock and rosemary together in a saucepan until just boiling. Season.

**6** Cut the dough into ravioli shapes. Cook in the boiling stock for about 2-4 minutes or until the pasta floats to the surface. Serve very hot in shallow soup plates.

# *Dolmades*

## INGREDIENTS

*225g/8oz fresh vine
leaves or leaves packed
in brine
8 spring onions
175g/6oz long-grain
rice, cooked
1½ tbsps chopped fresh
dill or fennel
3 tbsps chopped fresh
mint
1 tbsp chopped fresh
parsley
60g/2oz pine nuts
60g/2oz currants
Salt and pepper
140ml/¼pt olive oil
Juice of 1 lemon*

Step 3. Spread the leaves
out on a flat surface. Place
spoonfuls of stuffing on the
leaves and make into a
sausage shape.

## METHOD

❶ If using fresh vine leaves, put them into boiling water for about 1 minute. Remove them and drain. If using preserved vine leaves, rinse them and then place in a bowl of hot water for 5 minutes to soak. Drain and pat dry.

❷ Finely chop the spring onions and mix together with the rice, herbs, nuts and currants. Taste the filling and adjust the seasoning if necessary.

❸ Spread the vine leaves out on a flat surface, vein side upwards. Cut off the stems and place about 2 tsps of filling on each leaf, pressing it into a sausage shape.

❹ Fold the sides of the leaves over to partially cover the stuffing and roll up as for a Swiss roll. Place the rolls seam side down in a large saucepan. Pour over the olive oil and lemon juice.

❺ Pour hot water over the rolls until it comes about halfway up their sides. Place a plate on top of the rolls to keep them in place, cover the pan and cook slowly for about 40 minutes.

❻ Remove the dolmades to a serving plate and accompany with lemon wedges, black olives and plain yogurt if wished.

Preparation takes about
30 minutes, cooking
takes about 40 minutes.

Serves 6-8

Dolmades may be served
either hot or cold, and
are ideal for picnics.

# *Scallops with Fresh Basil*

Preparation takes about 15 minutes and cooking takes about 15 minutes.

Serves 6

Do not over-cook the scallops as they tend to become tough.

### INGREDIENTS

*4 small heads of chicory*
*120g/4oz butter*
*Salt and pepper*
*2 cloves garlic*
*10 fresh basil leaves*
*18 small scallops*

### METHOD

**1** Separate the chicory leaves and cut them lengthways into thin strips. Heat half the butter in a frying pan until foaming. Add the chicory and cook until quite tender. Add a little salt and pepper.

**2** Meanwhile, finely chop the garlic and basil leaves. Melt the remaining butter in a clean frying pan, add the garlic and basil and cook for 1 minute. Add the scallops to the pan and sauté on each side for 2-3 minutes or until just cooked through. Season to taste.

**3** Arrange the warm chicory on individual serving plates and place the scallops on top, pouring over any pan juices.

Step 2. Add the scallops to the garlic and basil and cook on each side for 2-3 minutes or until just cooked through.

# *Oregano Oysters*

## INGREDIENTS

*12 rashers bacon*
*15g/½oz butter*
*1 clove garlic*
*1 tbsp chopped parsley*
*1 tbsp chopped fresh oregano*
*1 tbsp Pernod*
*175ml/6 fl oz double cream*
*Salt and pepper*
*20 fresh oysters on the half shell*
*Coarse salt*

Step 4. Cook mixture until reduced by a quarter.

Step 5. Place the oysters in their shells into the coarse salt, twisting so that they stand level.

## METHOD

**1** Cook the bacon until crisp, then when cool finely crumble.

**2** Melt the butter or margarine in a saucepan. Crush the garlic, add to the pan and cook to soften, but not brown.

**3** Add the parsley, oregano, Pernod and cream. Bring to the boil and lower the heat to simmering. Strain on any liquid from the oysters and then loosen them from their shells with a small, sharp knife.

**4** Cook the mixture until reduced by about one quarter and slightly thickened. Test the seasoning and set the mixture aside.

**5** Pour about 1 inch coarse salt into a large roasting tin. Place the oysters on top of the salt and twist the shells into the salt so that they stand level.

**6** Spoon some of the cream over each oyster and sprinkle with the crumbled bacon. Bake in an oven preheated to 200°C/400°F/Gas Mark 6 for 15-18 minutes. Serve immediately.

Preparation takes about 25 minutes. Cooking takes about 20-25 minutes including time to cook the bacon.

Serves 4

# *Chicken Satay*

Preparation takes about 25 minutes, plus at least 1 hour marinating. Cooking takes about 15 minutes.

Serves 4

Use a selection of fresh vegetables instead of the chicken to make a vegetarian alternative.

## INGREDIENTS

**Marinade:**
2 tbsps soy sauce
2 tbsps sesame oil
2 tbsps lime juice
1 tsp ground cumin
1 tsp ground turmeric
2 tsps ground coriander

460g/1lb chicken breast
1 small onion
2 tbsps peanut oil
1 tsp chilli powder
120g/4oz crunchy peanut butter
1 tsp brown sugar

**Garnish:**
Lime wedges
Coriander leaves

## METHOD

**1** Put the marinade ingredients into a large bowl and mix well.

**2** Cut the chicken into 2.5cm/1-in cubes. Add to the marinade and stir well to coat the meat evenly. Cover with clingfilm and refrigerate for at least 1 hour, but preferably overnight.

**3** Drain the meat, reserving the marinade. Thread the meat onto 8 small skewers and set aside.

**4** Chop the onion very finely. Heat the peanut oil in a small saucepan and add the onion and chilli powder. Cook gently until the onion is slightly softened.

**5** Stir the reserved marinade into the oil and onion mixture, along with the peanut butter and brown sugar. Heat gently, stirring constantly, until all the ingredients are well blended. If the sauce is too thick, stir in 2-4 tbsps boiling water.

**6** Arrange the skewers of meat on a grill pan and cook under a preheated moderate grill for 10-15 minutes. After the first 5 minutes of cooking, brush the meat with a little of the peanut sauce to baste. Turn the meat frequently to cook it on all sides and prevent it browning. Garnish with the lime and coriander leaves, and serve the remaining sauce separately.

Step 3. Thread the marinated meat onto 8 small kebab skewers.

# *Countryside Terrine*

INGREDIENTS

*460g/1lb pig liver*
*340g/12oz lean pork*
*1 clove garlic*
*2 shallots*
*225g/8oz sausage meat*
*3 tbsps Cognac*
*½ tsp ground allspice*
*Salt and pepper*
*1 tsp chopped fresh thyme or sage*
*225g/8oz streaky bacon*
*120g/4oz smoked ham*
*2 tbsps double cream*
*1 large bay leaf*

METHOD

**1** Mince the liver and pork, crush the garlic and finely chop the shallots. Mix in a large bowl, together with the sausage meat, Cognac, allspice, salt and pepper and thyme.

**2** Stretch the bacon with a knife. Line a 900g/2lb loaf tin evenly with the bacon, overlapping each rasher slightly.

**3** Cut the ham into 5mm/1¼-in cubes and add to the pork with the cream, blending with your hands to keep the texture coarse. Press the mixture into the loaf tin, spreading it evenly. Place the bay leaf on the top and fold over any edges of bacon. Cover with a tight-fitting lid or two layers of foil.

**4** Stand the loaf tin in a roasting tin and pour water around it to come halfway up the sides of the loaf tin. Bake in an oven preheated to 180°C/350°F/Gas Mark 4 for 2 hours, or until the juices run clear when a knife is inserted into the centre. Remove the lid or foil and replace this with some fresh foil.

**5** Weigh down the terrine with cans of food or scale weights. Allow to cool, then refrigerate overnight, still weighted, until completely chilled and firm.

**6** To serve, remove the weights and foil and carefully turn the terrine out onto a serving plate. Scrape away any fat or jelly on the outside of the terrine, and cut into slices.

Step 2. Line a 900g/2lb loaf tin evenly with the bacon, overlapping each rasher slightly.

Preparation takes about 25 minutes, plus refrigeration time. Cooking takes about 2 hours.

Serves 6-8

This recipe will freeze well for up to 3 months. It should be packed in clingfilm, then a freezer bag and not aluminium foil.

# Pasta and Asparagus Salad

Preparation takes about 15 minutes, plus cooling. Cooking takes about 20 minutes.

Serves 4

Put the ingredients for the dressing into a screw top jar and shake vigorously to blend thoroughly.

## INGREDIENTS

*120g/4oz tagliatelle*
*460g/1lb asparagus*
*2 courgettes*
*2 lemons*
*2 tbsps chopped fresh parsley*
*2 tbsps chopped fresh marjoram*
*90ml/6 tbsps olive oil*
*Pinch of sugar*
*Salt and pepper*
*Lettuce to serve*

## METHOD

**1** Cook the pasta in plenty of lightly salted boiling water for 10 minutes or as directed on the packet. Drain and refresh in cold water. Drain again and leave to cool completely.

**2** Trim the asparagus and cut into 2.5cm/1-in pieces. Cut the courgettes into 5cm/2-in sticks. Cook the asparagus in lightly salted boiling water for 4 minutes, then add the courgettes and cook for a further 3-4 minutes or until the vegetables are just tender. Drain and refresh in cold water. Drain again and leave to cool.

**3** Cut off all the peel and white pith off 1 of the lemons then segment the flesh, cutting between the membranes. Place the cooked pasta, vegetables, herbs and lemon segments into a large bowl and mix together, taking care not to break up the vegetables.

**4** Mix together the oil, sugar and salt and pepper, to make the dressing. Grate the rind from the remaining lemon then squeeze the juice. Add to the dressing ingredients and blend together well with a fork or whisk.

**5** Arrange the lettuce on serving plates. Just before serving pour the dressing over the vegetables and pasta and mix gently to coat well. Pile equal quantities of the pasta salad into the centre of the lettuce and serve immediately.

Step 5. Stir the lemon and oil dressing into the pasta and vegetables, taking great care not to break up any of the ingredients.

# *Seviche*

## INGREDIENTS

*460g/1lb fresh cod fillet*
*2 limes*
*1 small shallot*
*1 green chilli*
*1 tsp ground coriander*
*1 small green pepper*
*1 small red pepper*
*4 spring onions*
*1 tbsp chopped fresh parsley*
*1 tbsp chopped fresh coriander*
*2 tbsps olive oil*
*Salt and pepper*
*1 small lettuce*

## METHOD

**1** Carefully remove the skin from the cod fillets. Using a sharp knife cut the fish into very thin strips across the grain.

**2** Grate the rind from the limes then squeeze the juice. Finely chop the shallot and chilli, removing the seeds as well.

**3** Put the fish strips into a large bowl and pour over the lime juice. Stir in the grated lime rind, shallot, chilli and ground coriander. Mix well.

**4** Cover the bowl with clingfilm and refrigerate for 24 hours, stirring occasionally.

**5** Slice the green and red peppers into strips and finely chop the spring onions. Mix in a large bowl together with the fresh herbs.

**6** Put the fish mixture into a colander and drain off the juice. Add the drained fish to the pepper mixture and stir in the oil, mixing well to coat evenly. Add salt and pepper to taste.

**7** Finely shred the lettuce and arrange on a serving plate. Spread the fish mixture attractively over the lettuce and serve immediately, garnished with slices of lime, if liked.

Step 1. Using a sharp knife, carefully remove the skin from the cod fillets.

Preparation takes 20 minutes plus 24 hours marinating time.

Serves 4

Use hake or salmon in place of the cod in this recipe.

# *Swedish Herrings*

Preparation takes 10 minutes, cooking takes 12-15 minutes.

Serves 4

To be sure that the fish you are buying are completely fresh, check that the skins are moist and the eyes are bright.

## INGREDIENTS

*60ml/4 tbsps chopped fresh dill*
*90ml/3 fl oz mild Swedish mustard*
*2 tbsps lemon juice or white wine*
*4-8 whole herrings, cleaned*
*30g/1oz unsalted butter, melted*
*Salt and pepper*
***Garnish:***
*Fresh dill*
*Lemon wedges*

## METHOD

❶ Put the dill, mustard and lemon juice or white wine into a small bowl and mix together thoroughly.

❷ Using a sharp knife, cut three shallow slits through the skin on both sides of each fish.

❸ Spread half of the mustard mixture over one side of each fish, pushing some of the mixture into each cut.

❹ Drizzle half the melted butter over the fish and grill under a preheated hot grill for 5-6 minutes.

❺ Using a fish slice, carefully turn each fish over, and spread with the remaining dill and mustard mixture.

❻ Drizzle over the remaining butter and grill for a further 5-6 minutes, or until the fish is thoroughly cooked.

❼ Sprinkle the fish with salt and pepper and serve garnished with the dill sprigs and lemon wedges.

Step 3. Spread the mustard mixture over each fish, carefully pushing a little into each cut.

# Monkfish and Pepper Kebabs

## INGREDIENTS

8 rashers of lean bacon
460g/1lb monkfish
1 small green pepper
1 small red pepper
12 small mushrooms
8 bay leaves
3 tbsps vegetable oil
2 shallots
120ml/4 fl oz dry white wine
60ml/4 tbsps tarragon vinegar
1 tbsp chopped fresh tarragon
1 tbsp chopped fresh chervil
225g/8oz butter, softened
Salt and pepper

## METHOD

**1** Remove the rind from the bacon then cut the rashers in half lengthways and then again in half crossways. Remove any membrane from the monkfish then cut into 2.5cm/1-in cubes. Cut the peppers into 2.5cm/1-in pieces.

**2** Put a piece of the fish onto each piece of bacon and roll the bacon around the piece of fish. Thread the rolls onto large skewers, alternating them with the peppers, mushrooms and the bay leaves.

**3** Brush the kebabs with the oil and arrange on a grill pan. Preheat the grill to hot and cook the kebabs for 10-15 minutes, turning them frequently to prevent the kebabs from burning.

**4** Finely chop the shallots and place in a small saucepan with the white wine and vinegar. Heat until boiling, then cook rapidly to reduce by half. Add the herbs and lower the heat.

**5** Using a small whisk beat the butter bit by bit into the hot wine mixture, whisking rapidly until the sauce becomes thick. Season to taste.

**6** Arrange the kebabs on a serving plate and serve with a little of the sauce spooned over and the remainder in a separate jug.

Step 2. Wrap each piece of fish in one of the strips of bacon.

Preparation takes 30 minutes, cooking will take about 25 minutes.

Serves 4

When making the sauce it is important to whisk briskly, or it will not thicken sufficiently.

# Trout with Chive Sauce

Preparation takes 15 minutes and cooking takes 15-20 minutes.

Serves 4

The chive sauce could also be served with grilled or poached salmon.

### INGREDIENTS

4 even-sized rainbow
trout, cleaned
Seasoned flour
60g/2oz butter, melted
2 tbsps white wine
280ml/½ pt double
cream
1 small bunch chives
Salt and pepper

### METHOD

**1** Dredge the trout with the seasoned flour and place in a lightly greased shallow baking tin. Spoon the hot melted butter over the fish.

**2** Place in an oven preheated to 200°C/400°F/Gas Mark 6 and bake for about 10 minutes, basting frequently with the butter. Cook until the skin is crisp.

**3** Test the fish on the underside close to the bone. If the fish is not cooked through, lower the oven temperature to 160°C/325°F Gas Mark 3 and cook for a further 5 minutes.

**4** Pour the wine into a small saucepan and bring to the boil. Boil to reduce by half. Pour in the cream and bring back to the boil. Allow to boil rapidly until the cream thickens slightly.

**5** Cut up the chives using a pair of scissors. Stir the snipped chives into the sauce, reserving some to sprinkle on top, if wished.

**6** When the fish are browned, remove to a serving dish and spoon over some of the sauce. Sprinkle with the reserved chives and serve the rest of the sauce separately.

# *Swordfish Steaks with Green Peppercorns and Garlic Sauce*

## INGREDIENTS

*2 tbsps fresh green peppercorns*
*90ml/6 tbsps lemon juice*
*60ml/4 tbsps olive oil*
*Salt*
*4 swordfish steaks*
*1 clove garlic*
*1 egg*
*140ml/¼ pt oil*
*2 tsps fresh chopped oregano leaves*

## METHOD

**1** Crush the green peppercorns lightly using a pestle and mortar. Mix in the lemon juice, olive oil and some salt.

**2** Place the swordfish steaks in a shallow ovenproof dish and pour the lemon and oil mixture over each steak. Refrigerate overnight, turning occasionally until the fish becomes opaque.

**3** Roughly chop the garlic and, using a blender or food processor, mix together with the egg. With the machine still running, gradually pour the oil through the funnel in a thin steady stream onto the egg and garlic mixture. Continue to blend until the sauce is thick.

**4** Arrange the swordfish on a grill pan and sprinkle over the oregano. Cook under a preheated hot grill for 15 minutes, turning them frequently and basting with the lemon and pepper marinade.

**5** When the steaks are cooked, place onto a serving dish and spoon the garlic mayonnaise over to serve.

Step 1. Lightly crush the green peppercorns using a pestle and mortar.

Step 2. Marinate the swordfish steaks overnight, after such time they should be opaque.

Preparation takes 25 minutes, plus overnight soaking. Cooking takes about 15 minutes.

Serves 4

Substitute 2 tbsps well rinsed canned green peppercorns in place of the fresh peppercorns if you cannot get these, and use tuna steaks instead of the swordfish if you prefer.

# *Tarragon Grilled Red Mullet*

Preparation takes about 15 minutes, cooking takes 10-16 minutes.

Serves 4

Use herrings or mackerel in place of the mullet.

## INGREDIENTS

*4 large red mullet, cleaned and scaled*
*4 sprigs of fresh tarragon*
*60ml/4 tbsps olive oil*
*2 tbsps tarragon vinegar*
*Salt and pepper*
*1 egg*
*1 tsp Dijon mustard*
*120ml/4 fl oz sunflower oil*
*1 tbsp wine vinegar*
*1 tsp brandy*
*1 tbsp chopped fresh tarragon*
*1 tbsp chopped fresh parsley*
*1 tbsp double cream*

## METHOD

1. Rub the inside of each mullet with salt, scrubbing hard to remove any membranes. Rinse thoroughly.

2. Place a sprig of fresh tarragon inside each fish. Using a sharp knife cut 2 diagonal slits on each side of all the fish.

3. Mix together the olive oil, tarragon vinegar and a little salt and pepper in a small bowl.

4. Arrange the fish in a shallow dish and pour over the tarragon vinegar marinade, brushing some of the mixture into the cuts on the side of the fish. Refrigerate for 30 minutes.

5. Put the egg into a blender or food processor along with the mustard and a little salt and pepper. Process for 2-3 seconds to mix. With the machine running, add the oil in a thin stream. Continue blending until thick and creamy. Add the vinegar, brandy and herbs, and process for 30 seconds.

6. Lightly whip the cream until it thickens. Fold carefully into the dressing. Refrigerate until ready to use.

7. Arrange the fish on a grill pan and cook under a hot grill for about 6-8 minutes per side, depending on the size of the fish. Baste frequently with the marinade. Serve with the sauce.

# *Szechuan Fish*

## INGREDIENTS

460g/1lb white fish
fillets
Salt and pepper
1 egg
38g/5 tbsps flour
90ml/6 tbsps white
wine
Oil for deep-frying
60g/2oz cooked ham
2.5cm/1-in fresh ginger
6 water chestnuts
4 spring onions
½-1 red or green chilli
3 tbsps light soy sauce
1 tsp cider vinegar
½ tsp ground Szechuan
pepper
1 tbsp cornflour
2 tbsps water
280ml/½ pt light stock
2 tsps sugar
**Garnish:**
Fresh chillies

## METHOD

**1** Cut the fish fillets into 5cm/2-in pieces and season. Beat the egg well and add the flour and wine to make a batter.

**2** Heat a wok and when hot, add enough oil to deep-fry the fish. When the oil is hot, dredge the fish lightly with some flour and then dip a few pieces of fish into the batter, mixing well. Add to the hot oil and fry until golden brown. Drain and proceed until all the fish is cooked. Allow the oil to cool.

**3** Cut the ham into small dice and finely dice the ginger and water chestnuts. Finely chop the spring onions and deseed and finely dice the chilli.

**4** Remove all but 1 tbsp of oil from the wok and add the ham, ginger, diced chilli, water chestnuts and spring onions. Cook for about 1 minute and add the soy sauce, vinegar and Szechuan pepper. Stir well and cook for a further 1 minute. Remove the vegetables from the pan and set them aside.

**5** Blend the cornflour with the water. Add the stock to the wok and bring to the boil. When boiling, add 1 spoonful of the hot stock to the cornflour mixture. Add the mixture back to the stock and reboil, stirring constantly until thickened.

**6** Stir in the sugar and return the fish and vegetables to the sauce. Heat through for 30 seconds and serve garnished with chillies.

Preparation takes about 30 minutes. Cooking takes about 10 minutes.

Serves 6

Serve with plain or fried rice. Do not eat the chilli garnish.

# *Sea Bream with Peppercorn Sauce*

Preparation takes 20 minutes and cooking takes about 30 minutes.

Serves 4

Serve with baby new potatoes and mange tout peas or French beans.

## INGREDIENTS

*1 tomato*
*2 shallots*
*1 tbsp olive oil*
*10 green peppercorns*
*10 pink peppercorns*
*1 tbsp Cognac*
*1 sherry glass of aniseed alcohol*
*140ml/¼ pt white wine*
*1 tbsp sugar*
*2 large black sea bream, cleaned, scaled and filleted*
*280ml/½ pt double cream*
**Garnish:**
*Sprigs of chervil*

## METHOD

**1** Skin, deseed and finely chop the tomato. Finely chop the shallots. Heat the olive oil in a frying pan and sauté both types of peppercorns until aromatic.

**2** Drain off the oil from the pan and deglaze with the Cognac. Add the tomato, shallots, aniseed alcohol, wine and sugar. Stir well and cook until the mixture reduces, thickens and becomes quite syrupy. This may take a while if the tomato is very juicy.

**3** Meanwhile, cut the fish fillets crossways into strips about 4cm/1½-in wide. When the sauce is just about ready place the fish on a grill pan and brush with a little oil. Place under a preheated medium hot grill and cook for about 2 minutes on each side, or until the fish is cooked through. The exact cooking time will depend on the thickness of the fish.

**4** Add the cream to the sauce and whisk over a gentle heat. Arrange the fish on warm serving plates then pour the sauce around the fish to serve. Garnish with sprigs of chervil.

# *Turkey Kebabs*

## INGREDIENTS

*1.25kg/3lbs lean
turkey meat*
*2 tsps fresh sage*
*1 sprig rosemary*
*Juice of 1 lemon*
*2 tbsps olive oil*
*Salt and pepper*
*120g/4oz lean back
bacon*
*Whole sage leaves*

## METHOD

**1** Cut the turkey meat into even-sized cubes. Chop the sage and rosemary leaves very finely. Put the chopped sage, rosemary, lemon juice, oil, salt and pepper into a large bowl and stir in the turkey meat, mixing well to coat evenly. Cover and leave in the refrigerator overnight.

**2** Cut the rind off the bacon and cut the bacon rashers in half lengthways and then again crossways. Wrap these pieces around as many of the cubes of marinated turkey meat as possible. Thread the turkey and bacon rolls alternately with the sage leaves and any unwrapped turkey cubes onto kebab skewers.

**3** Heat a grill to moderate, and cook the kebabs under the heat for about 15 minutes, or until the meat is cooked through. Turn frequently and baste with the marinade whilst cooking. Serve immediately.

Step 2. Carefully roll pieces of the marinated turkey in the rashers of bacon.

Preparation takes about 10 minutes, cooking takes about 15 minutes.

Serves 6

Serve with pitta bread and salad, or on a bed of rice.

# Rosemary Chicken Surprise

Preparation takes about 25 minutes and cooking takes about 45 minutes.

Serves 4

Add a pinch of saffron strands to the chicken stock for extra colour and flavour.

INGREDIENTS

8 chicken livers
3 tbsps fresh rosemary leaves
4 large chicken legs, boned
Salt and pepper
570ml/1 pt rich chicken stock
60g/2oz butter
Fresh spaghetti to serve

METHOD

**1** Trim the chicken livers and rinse them in plenty of cold water. Chop the rosemary very finely.

**2** Spread the chicken meat on a work surface, skin side down. Sprinkle the inside of the meat with salt, pepper and 2 tbsps of the rosemary.

**3** Place the chicken livers over the seasoning, roll the meat tightly around the liver and secure each well with kitchen string.

**4** Heat the chicken stock with the remaining rosemary and add the chicken rolls. Cover and simmer gently for 20 minutes. Remove the chicken rolls and keep them warm.

**5** Place the saucepan back on a high heat and boil the sauce rapidly to reduce and thicken. Reduce the heat to very low and whisk in the butter, piece by piece. Do not allow the sauce to boil.

**6** Cut the chicken rolls into slices and serve on a bed of hot spaghetti with the sauce poured over.

Step 3. Roll up the chicken and secure well with kitchen string.

# Pan-Fried Crispy Chicken

## INGREDIENTS

4 chicken breasts
2 egg whites
60g/8 tbsps dry
breadcrumbs
1 tbsp chopped fresh
sage
Salt and pepper
2 tbsps walnut oil
120ml/4 fl oz
mayonnaise
140ml/¼ pt natural
yogurt
1 tsp grated fresh
horseradish
2 tbsps chopped
walnuts
**Garnish:**
Lemon slices
Chopped walnuts

## METHOD

**1** Bone and skin the chicken breasts and pat dry with kitchen paper. Whisk the egg whites with a fork until they just begin to froth, but are still liquid. Carefully brush all surfaces of the chicken breasts with the beaten egg white.

**2** Put the breadcrumbs onto a shallow plate and mix in the sage. Season with salt and pepper. Place the chicken breasts, one at a time, onto the plate of breadcrumbs and sage, and carefully press the mixture onto the chicken.

**3** Put the oil into a large shallow pan, and gently fry the prepared chicken breasts on each side for 6-8 minutes until they are lightly golden and tender. Set them aside, and keep warm.

**4** Mix all the remaining ingredients, except for the garnish, in a small bowl, whisking well to blend the yogurt and mayonnaise evenly.

**5** Place the chicken on serving plates, and spoon a little of the sauce over each. Serve garnished with the lemon slices and additional chopped nuts.

Step 2. Press the breadcrumb and sage mixture onto the chicken breasts, making sure that they are covered evenly.

Preparation takes about 20 minutes, cooking takes 10-15 minutes.

Serves 4

Use almonds instead of walnuts in this recipe, and limes instead of lemons. Oranges and hazelnuts make another delicious variation.

# Saffron Chicken

Preparation takes about
25 minutes, cooking
takes about 30-35
minutes.

Serves 4

Use ¼ tsp ground
saffron instead of saffron
threads and omit the
soaking with the boiling
water.

INGREDIENTS

2 tbsps olive oil
1.5kg/3 lb chicken,
jointed
Salt and pepper
1 small onion
1 clove garlic
2 tsps paprika pepper
8 tomatoes
275g/10oz long grain
white rice
700ml/1¼ pts boiling
water
Large pinch of saffron
strands
175g/6oz frozen peas
2 tbsps chopped fresh
parsley

METHOD

❶ Heat the oil in a large casserole and fry the chicken joints, turning them frequently to brown evenly. Season, then remove from the pan and set aside.

❷ Chop the onion finely and crush the garlic, add to the juices in the casserole and cook slowly until softened but not coloured. Add the paprika and fry gently for about 30 seconds.

❸ Skin, core and deseed the tomatoes. Chop the flesh finely and add to the casserole. Cook for about 5-10 minutes to draw off the liquid from the tomatoes. The sauce should be of a dropping consistency when done.

❹ Crush the saffron strands and mix with a little of the boiling water. Leave to stand for 10 minutes. Stir the rice, saffron and remaining water into the sauce along with the chicken. Bring to the boil, then cover the casserole tightly and simmer for about 20 minutes. Stir frequently to prevent the rice from sticking.

❺ Add the peas and the parsley to the casserole, stir well and continue cooking for a further 5-10 minutes, or until the rice is tender and all the liquid has been absorbed.

# *Chicken Cacciatore*

## INGREDIENTS

60ml/4 tbsps olive oil
1.5kg/3lbs chicken
pieces
2 onions
3 cloves garlic
225g/8oz button
mushrooms
140ml/¼ pt red wine
1 tbsp wine vinegar
1 tbsp fresh parsley
2 tsps fresh oregano
2 tsps fresh basil
1 bay leaf
460g/1lb canned
tomatoes
140ml/¼ pt chicken
stock
Black pepper
Pinch of sugar
60g/2oz black olives,
pitted

## METHOD

**1** Heat the oil in a large frying pan and add the chicken pieces, skin side down, in one layer. Brown for 3-4 minutes, then turn each piece over. Continue turning the chicken portions until all surfaces are well browned. Remove the chicken portions to a plate and keep warm.

**2** Slice the onions and crush the garlic and add to the oil and chicken juices in the frying pan. Cook lightly for 2-3 minutes, or until they are just beginning to brown. Quarter the mushrooms, add to the pan and cook for about 1 minute, stirring constantly. Pour the wine and vinegar into the pan and boil rapidly to reduce to about half the original quantity.

**3** Chop the parsley, oregano and basil and add to the pan with the bay leaf and tomatoes, stirring well to break up the tomatoes. Stir in the chicken stock and season with pepper and sugar. Return the chicken to the tomato sauce and cover with a tight fitting lid. Simmer for about 1 hour, or until the chicken is tender. Add the olives during the last 5 minutes of cooking.

Step 1. Turn the chicken frequently until all the outer surfaces are golden brown.

Preparation takes about 20 minutes, cooking takes 1¼ hours.

Serves 4-6

Serve with rice or pasta, and a mixed salad.

# 🌸 Roast Pigeon with 🌸 Juniper Sauce

Preparation takes 15 minutes and cooking takes 40-45 minutes.

Serves 2

Accompany with noodles or potatoes. Serving and eating are easier if the pigeons are cut in half first.

Step 1. Remove pin feathers with tweezers or singe the pigeons over an open flame.

## INGREDIENTS

2 pigeons, dressed
120g/4oz chicken liver pâté
1 tbsp brandy
6 rashers streaky bacon

**Sauce:**
60g/2oz smoked bacon
1 onion
½ carrot
1 stick celery
1 tbsp juniper berries
2 tbsps flour
280ml/½ pt brown stock
140ml/¼ pt white wine
1 tsp tomato purée (optional)
Salt and pepper

## METHOD

**1** Pluck any pin feathers from the pigeons with tweezers or singe them over a gas flame. Mix pâté and brandy together and spread on the insides of each pigeon.

**2** Tie the bacon on the pigeons to cover the breasts and roast them in an oven preheated to 200°C/400°F/Gas Mark 6 for 35-40 minutes.

**3** Meanwhile, make the sauce. Finely chop the bacon, onion, carrot and celery. Place the chopped bacon in a heavy-based saucepan over low heat and cook slowly.

**4** Add the vegetables and juniper berries and cook until the vegetables begin to brown lightly. Add the flour and cook over a low heat until golden brown, stirring to prevent the flour from burning.

**5** Pour on the stock gradually, stirring continuously. Bring to the boil and reduce the heat to simmer. Partially cover the pan and cook slowly for about 20-25 minutes. Add more stock or water as necessary.

**6** Skim off the fat from the roasting tin. Add pan juices to the sauce and pour in the juices from the cavity of each pigeon.

**7** Strain the sauce into a clean pan and add the wine and tomato purée, if using. Boil for about 3 minutes to reduce slightly. Season and serve with the pigeons.

# Herb-Roasted Guinea Fowl with Redcurrants

## INGREDIENTS

2 oven-ready guinea
fowl
30g/1oz softened butter
**Stuffing:**
3 shallots
45g/1½oz butter
1 tbsp chopped parsley
1 tbsp chopped
marjoram
1 tbsp chopped thyme
1 tsp chopped sage
1 tsp dried rosemary
175g/6oz fresh
breadcrumbs
Salt and pepper
**Sauce:**
1 tbsp red wine vinegar
280ml/½ pt chicken
stock
2 tbsps arrowroot
225g/8oz redcurrants,
stems removed
1 tbsp redcurrant jelly
Grated nutmeg
Salt and pepper
**Garnish:**
Fresh redcurrants
Herb sprigs

## METHOD

**1** Prepare the stuffing. Finely chop the shallots. Melt the butter in a pan. Add the shallots and cook until softened. Cool slightly. Stir in remaining stuffing ingredients.

**2** Loosen the skin on each guinea fowl. Divide the stuffing between the two birds and push up under the skin, spreading it out over the breast and thighs. Spread the softened butter evenly over each bird.

**3** Cook in a roasting tin in an oven preheated to 190ºC/375ºF/Gas Mark 5 for about 1 hour, basting 2 or 3 times with the pan juices. Allow to rest for 5 minutes before cutting in half to serve.

**4** To make the sauce, skim all but 1 tbsp of fat from the roasting tin, add the vinegar and heat to reduce slightly.

**5** Mix 2 tbsps of the chicken stock with the arrowroot. Add the remaining stock and redcurrants to the roasting tin. Crush the currants with a spoon.

**6** Bring to the boil and boil rapidly to reduce by a quarter. Stir in the redcurrant jelly. Stir some of the hot liquid into the arrowroot and add to the roasting tin. Stirring constantly, bring to the boil to thicken. Add some nutmeg, salt and pepper, and strain if preferred.

Preparation takes 30 minutes and cooking takes about 1 hour.

Serves 4

Use frozen or canned redcurrants if fresh ones are not available. If using canned redcurrants substitute some of the stock with the juice.

# Veal in Marjoram Sauce

Preparation takes about 10 minutes and cooking takes about 20 minutes.

Serves 4

A little butter can be whisked into the sauce to make it richer. Remove the meat at the end of Step 4 and whisk in small knobs of butter. Return the meat to the sauce before serving.

## INGREDIENTS

4 veal escalopes
Salt and pepper
Flour to coat
½ onion
2 large mushrooms
2 tbsps olive oil
1 clove garlic, chopped
1 tbsp fresh marjoram
2 tsps chopped parsley
175ml/6 fl oz chicken stock

## METHOD

**1** Trim the veal of any fat and cut across the grain into very thin slices. Season the slices with salt and pepper and toss in flour to coat. Shake off any excess flour.

**2** Finely chop the onion and cut the mushrooms into very thin slices. Heat the oil in a frying pan and gently fry the onion, mushrooms and garlic for a few minutes.

**3** Add the thin slices of veal, marjoram and parsley. Stir and turn the slices of meat over once.

**4** Stir in the stock and bring to the boil, reduce the heat and cook until the sauce thickens. Shake and stir the contents of the pan occasionally. Taste and adjust seasoning and serve hot.

Step 1. Cut the veal escalopes crossways into very thin slices.

# *Roast Pork Wild Game Style*

## INGREDIENTS

1.5kg/3lb boneless
pork joint
60g/2oz lard
Paprika
1 tsp flour
175ml/6 fl oz soured
cream
1 tbsp chopped dill
**Marinade:**
1 carrot
2 sticks celery
2 onions, chopped
10 juniper berries
1 lemon
140ml/ ¼ pt white
wine
1 bay leaf
5 black peppercorns
5 allspice berries
2 sprigs of thyme
**Accompaniment:**
900g/2lbs cooked
beetroot, peeled
1 onion
1 clove garlic, crushed
60g/2oz butter
2 tbsps flour
140ml/¼ pt chicken
stock
Sugar
White wine vinegar
Salt and pepper

## METHOD

**1** Prepare the marinade. Finely chop the carrot and celery and lightly crush the juniper berries. Grate the lemon rind and squeeze the juice. Combine with the rest of the marinade in a pan and bring to the boil. Remove from the heat and cool. Put the pork in a bowl and pour over the marinade. Cover and refrigerate for 2 days, turning the meat often. Remove the meat and dry it. Reserve the marinade.

**2** Heat the lard in a roasting tin. Sprinkle the pork rind with paprika, and brown all over. Cook in an oven preheated to 190°C/ 375°F/Gas Mark 5 for 1 hour. Pour over the marinade and cook for a further 1-1¼ hours, or until tender, basting frequently.

**3** Remove the pork from the pan. Skim off any fat from the sauce. Mix the flour, soured cream and dill together and add to the pan. Bring just to the boil, then simmer for 1-2 minutes.

**4** Grate the beetroot and finely chop the onion. Melt the butter in a pan and add the flour and onion. Stir well and cook gently until light brown. Add the garlic and gradually stir in the stock. Bring to the boil, add the beetroot and sugar, vinegar and seasoning to taste. Simmer for 10 minutes, stirring occasionally. To serve, slice the pork and pour over the sauce. Serve with the beetroot.

Preparation takes about 40 minutes plus 2 days marinating. Cooking takes 2-2¼ hours for the pork and about 10 minutes for the beetroot.

Serves 6

The beetroot will lose its colour if it is overcooked or reheated so make the accompaniment just before serving.

# Roast Pork with Caraway Seeds

Preparation takes about 20 minutes and cooking takes about 1¼ hours.

Serves 6

Step 2. Score the fat in a diamond pattern, and sprinkle with salt, marjoram and caraway seeds.

## INGREDIENTS

900g/2lb pork joint
Salt
Marjoram
2 tsps caraway seeds
1½ tbsps oil
2 onions
280ml/½ pt stock

## METHOD

❶ Remove the rind of the pork in one piece, leaving most of the fat on the joint. Place the rind in a shallow pan, brush lightly with oil and sprinkle with salt.

❷ Score the fat of the joint in a diamond pattern. Sprinkle with salt, a pinch of marjoram and the caraway seeds. Leave to stand in the refrigerator for at least 1 hour before cooking.

❸ Heat the oil in a roasting tin and brown the meat, fat side down first. Cook on all sides and then turn over fat side down again. Add the onions and stock.

❹ Roast in an oven preheated to 220°C/425°F/Gas Mark 7 for 30 minutes. Turn over and continue roasting for 45 minutes or until the juices run clear, basting frequently with the cooking liquid. Cook the rind at the same time in a separate tin, turning it over halfway through the cooking time.

❺ Carve the joint into slices or take to the table whole. Skim the fat from the surface of the pan juices and reduce them slightly if necessary by boiling over a high heat. Pour around the meat to serve. Carve the crackling and serve with the pork.

# Paprika Pork Escalopes

## INGREDIENTS

*8 thin pork escalopes*
*Salt and pepper*
*1 clove garlic*
*3 tbsps vegetable oil*
*1 onion*
*1 red pepper*
*1 green pepper*
*1 tbsp paprika*
*140ml/¼ pt beef stock*
*120ml/4 fl oz red wine*
*3 tbsps tomato purée*
*140ml/¼ pt natural yogurt*

## METHOD

1. If necessary, flatten out the pork escalopes with a rolling pin until they are 5mm/¼-in thick. Rub both sides of the pork with salt, pepper and garlic, then refrigerate for 30 minutes.

2. Heat the oil in a large frying pan, and cook the pork in several batches if necessary, until well browned and cooked right through. This will take about 3-4 minutes on each side. Remove the pork from the pan and keep warm.

3. Thinly slice the onion into rings and slice the peppers lengthways into thin strips. Add the onion and peppers to the pan and cook quickly for about 3-4 minutes until soft but not browned.

4. Add the paprika, stock, wine and tomato purée to the pan and bring to the boil. Reduce the heat and simmer until the liquid has evaporated and the sauce has thickened. Season to taste.

5. Arrange the escalopes on a serving dish and pour the sauce over the top of them.

6. Beat the yogurt until it is smooth. Carefully drizzle the yogurt over the paprika sauce to make an attractive pattern. Swirl gently into the sauce to blend, but take care not to incorporate it completely. Serve hot.

Step 3. Fry the onions and peppers together for 3-4 minutes until they have softened but not browned.

Preparation takes 30 minutes and cooking takes about 20 minutes.

Serves 4

If the yogurt is too thick to drizzle properly, whisk in a little water or milk to thin it to the required consistency.

# ❀ *Spiced Lamb* ❀

Preparation takes about 25 minutes, plus 4 hours marinating time for the meat. Cooking takes about 35 minutes.

Serves 4

Serve with rice or baby new potatoes.

### INGREDIENTS

*460g/1lb lamb neck fillet*
*1 tsp chopped fresh dill*
*1 tsp finely chopped rosemary leaves*
*1 tsp chopped thyme*
*2 tsps mustard seeds*
*2 bay leaves*
*1 tsp black pepper*
*½ tsp ground allspice*
*Juice of 2 lemons*
*280ml/½ pt red wine*
*1 small red pepper*
*2 tbsps oil*
*90g/3oz button mushrooms*
*30g/1oz butter or margarine*
*3 tbsps flour*
*140ml/¼ pt beef stock*
*Salt*

### METHOD

**1** Place the lamb in a shallow dish and sprinkle on the dill, rosemary, thyme and lightly crushed mustard seeds. Add the bay leaves, pepper, allspice, lemon juice and wine, and stir to coat the meat thoroughly with the marinade. Leave for 4 hours in the refrigerator.

**2** Slice the red pepper. Heat the oil in a large frying pan and add the pepper and whole mushrooms and cook to soften slightly. Remove with a draining spoon.

**3** Reheat the oil in the pan and add the lamb fillet, well drained and patted dry. Reserve the marinade. Brown the meat quickly on all sides to seal. Remove from the pan and set aside with the vegetables.

**4** Melt the butter in the pan and when foaming add the flour. Lower the heat and cook the flour slowly until a good, rich brown. Gradually stir in the beef stock and the marinade. Bring to the boil and return the vegetables and lamb to the pan. Cook for about 15 minutes, or until the lamb is tender, but still pink inside.

**5** Slice the lamb fillet thinly on the diagonal and arrange on plates. Remove the bay leaves from the sauce and spoon over the meat to serve.

Step 5. To serve, slice lamb fillet on the diagonal with a large, sharp knife or carving knife.

# Leg of Lamb with Chilli Sauce

## INGREDIENTS

1kg/2¼lb leg of lamb
1 tbsp cornflour
**Marinade:**
1 tsp cocoa powder
¼ tsp cayenne pepper
½ tsp ground cumin
½ tsp paprika
½ tsp chopped oregano
140ml/¼ pt water
140ml/¼ pt orange juice
140ml/¼ pt red wine
1 clove garlic
2 tbsps brown sugar
Pinch of salt
**Garnish:**
Orange slices
Coriander sprigs

## METHOD

1. Trim the lamb of surface fat and remove the paper-thin skin if possible. Place lamb in a shallow dish.

2. Mix together the marinade ingredients and pour over the lamb, turning it well to coat completely. Cover and refrigerate for 12-24 hours, turning occasionally.

3. Drain the lamb, reserving the marinade, and place in a roasting tin. Cook in an oven preheated to 180°C/350°F/Gas Mark 4 for about 2 hours, or until meat is cooked according to taste. Baste occasionally with the marinade and pan juices.

4. Remove the lamb to a serving dish and keep warm. Skim the fat from the top of the roasting tin with a large spoon and discard.

5. Pour the remaining marinade into the juices in the roasting tin and bring to the boil, stirring to scrape up the browned juice. Mix the cornflour with a small amount of water and add some of the liquid from the roasting tin. Gradually stir the cornflour mixture into the tin and bring back to the boil.

6. Cook, stirring constantly, until thickened and clear. Add more orange juice, wine or water if necessary.

7. Garnish the lamb with orange slices and sprigs of coriander. Pour over some of the sauce and serve the rest separately.

Step 6. Cook, stirring constantly, until thickened and clear. Add more orange juice, wine or water if necessary.

Preparation takes about 15 minutes, plus 12-24 hours for the lamb to marinate. Cooking takes about 2 hours for the lamb and 20 minutes to finish the sauce.

Serves 4

The marinade ingredients can also be used with beef or poultry.

# Lamb Korma

Preparation takes about 15 minutes, and cooking takes about 45-50 minutes.

Serves 4

Serve with boiled rice, or chapatis.

## INGREDIENTS

460g/1lb shoulder of lamb
1 medium onion
3 tbsps vegetable oil
2.5cm/1-in piece cinnamon stick
6 cloves
Seeds of 6 green cardamoms
1 bay leaf
1 tsp black cumin seeds
2 tsps grated fresh ginger
2 cloves garlic, crushed
1 tsp chilli powder
1 tsp ground coriander
2 tsps ground cumin
¼ tsp ground turmeric
140ml/¼ pt natural yogurt
160ml/6 fl oz water
Salt to taste
2 green chillies
2 sprigs fresh coriander
1 tbsp ground almonds

## METHOD

1 Trim the lamb and cut into cubes. Slice the onion. Heat the oil in a large frying pan, add the onion and cook until golden brown. Add the cinnamon, cloves, cardamoms, bay leaf and cumin seeds and fry for 1 minute.

2 Add the ginger and garlic and the cubed lamb. Sprinkle over the chilli powder, ground coriander, cumin and turmeric and mix together well.

3 Stir in the yogurt, cover the pan and cook over a moderate heat for 10-15 minutes, stirring occasionally.

4 Add the water and salt to taste, re-cover and simmer gently for 30-40 minutes, or until the meat is tender.

5 Halve and deseed the chillies and chop the coriander leaves. Just before serving, add the almonds, chillies and coriander leaves. Stir in a little more water, if necessary, to produce a medium-thick gravy.

# *Boiled Beef*

## INGREDIENTS

1.5kg/3lb corned
silverside or brisket
1 bay leaf
1 tsp mustard seed
3 allspice berries
3 cloves
1 tsp dill seed
6 black peppercorns
2 large potatoes
4 small onions
4 large carrots
4 small or 2 large
parsnips
1 large or 2 small
swedes
1 medium cabbage
Salt

## METHOD

**1** Place the beef in a large casserole with enough water to cover and add the bay leaf and spices. Cook for about 2 hours, skimming any foam from the surface as the meat cooks.

**2** Cut the potatoes and onions into even-size pieces, add to the casserole and cook for about 15 minutes. Taste and add salt if necessary.

**3** Add the carrots, whole, and the parsnips and swede cut into pieces and cook for a further 15 minutes. Quarter the cabbage, add to the casserole and cook a further 15 minutes.

**4** When the meat is tender, remove it from the casserole and slice it thinly. Arrange on a warm serving platter and remove the vegetables from the broth with a draining spoon, placing them around the meat. Serve immediately with horseradish or mustard.

Step 3. When the beef and root vegetables have cooked for 15 minutes, add the cabbage, pushing it under the liquid.

Preparation takes about 30 minutes and cooking takes about 3 hours.

Serves 4-6

# *Spiced Beef*

Preparation takes about 30 minutes and cooking takes 5-6 minutes.

Serves 4

For a variation, add 120g/4oz sliced button mushrooms and 225g/8oz cooked Chinese egg noodles.

## INGREDIENTS

*460g/1lb fillet of beef*
*2.5cm/1-in fresh ginger*
*6 spring onions*
*1 tsp soft brown sugar*
*2-3 star anise, ground*
*½ tsp ground fennel seeds*
*1 tbsp dark soy sauce*
*½ tsp salt*
*2 tbsps vegetable oil*
*1 tbsp light soy sauce*
*½ tsp black pepper*

Step 3. Put the sliced beef, ginger and salt into the marinade and stir well to coat evenly.

Step 5. Stir fry the beef with the spring onions for 4 minutes.

## METHOD

**1** Cut the beef into thin strips 2.5cm/1-in long. Grate the ginger and slice the spring onions.

**2** In a bowl, mix together the sugar, spices and dark soy sauce.

**3** Put the beef, ginger and salt into the soy sauce mixture and stir well to coat evenly. Cover and allow to stand for 20 minutes.

**4** Heat the oil in a wok and stir-fry the onions quickly for 1 minute.

**5** Add the beef and fry, stirring constantly, for 4 minutes, or until the meat is well browned.

**6** Stir in the light soy sauce and black pepper and cook gently for a further 1 minute.

# *Chilli con Carne*

## INGREDIENTS

*1 tbsp oil*
*460g/1lb minced beef*
*2 tsps ground cumin*
*2 tsps mild or hot chilli*
*powder*
*Pinch of oregano*
*Salt and pepper*
*Pinch of sugar*
*1 clove garlic, crushed*
*2 tbsps flour*
*460g/1lb canned*
*tomatoes*
*460g/1lb canned red*
*kidney beans*

## METHOD

**1** Heat the oil in a large saucepan and brown the meat, breaking it up with a fork as it cooks. Sprinkle on the cumin, chilli powder, oregano, salt and pepper, sugar, garlic and flour. Cook, stirring frequently, over a medium heat for about 3 minutes.

**2** Add the tomatoes and their liquid, stir in well and break up the tomatoes with the back of a spoon. Cover and simmer for 25-30 minutes.

**3** Drain the kidney beans and add just before serving. Heat through for about 5 minutes.

Step 2. Add the tomatoes and their liquid. Use a large spoon or potato masher to break up the tomatoes.

Preparation takes about 15 minutes. Cooking takes about 40 minutes.

Serves 4

Spoon the chilli on top of boiled rice to serve. Top with soured cream, chopped spring onion, grated cheese, diced avocado or a combination of the four ingredients.

# Egg Curry

Preparation takes about 10 minutes, and cooking takes 20 minutes.

Serves 4

If a milder curry is preferred, reduce the amount of chilli powder to ½ tsp and carefully remove the seeds from the green chillies before you chop them.

### INGREDIENTS

4-6 eggs
1 large onion
1 tbsp oil
2.5cm/1-in stick cinnamon
1 bay leaf
4 green cardamoms
6 cloves
1 tsp grated fresh ginger
1 clove garlic, crushed
1 tsp ground coriander
1 tsp ground cumin
¼ tsp ground turmeric
1 tsp garam masala
1 tsp chilli powder
225g/8oz canned tomatoes
Salt
175ml/6 fl oz water or vegetable stock
2 sprigs fresh coriander leaves
2 green chillies

Step 5. Put the hard-boiled eggs into the curry sauce, stir well and cook for 10-12 minutes.

### METHOD

❶ Hard-boil the eggs in boiling water for 8-10 minutes. Cool them completely in cold water, then remove the shells.

❷ Peel the onion and chop it finely. Heat the oil in a large saucepan and fry the onion gently for 2-3 minutes until it is soft, but not browned.

❸ Add the cinnamon, bay leaf, cardamoms and cloves and fry for 1 minute. Stir in the ginger and garlic. Add the coriander, cumin, turmeric, garam masala and chilli powder. Stir together well and fry for 30 seconds.

❹ Crush the tomatoes and add to the pan. Stir in well, season and simmer for 5 minutes. Add the water or stock and bring the mixure to the boil.

❺ Put the eggs into the curry sauce and simmer for 10-12 minutes.

❻ Chop the coriander leaves and the green chillies finely and sprinkle them over the cooked eggs, to garnish.

# *Pasta with Fresh Basil Sauce*

## INGREDIENTS

*460g/1lb fresh pasta*
*20 fresh basil leaves*
*1 clove garlic*
*2 tbsps grated Parmesan*
*60ml/2 fl oz olive oil*
*30g/1oz butter*
*Salt and pepper*

## METHOD

**1** Cook the pasta according to packet instructions in salted, boiling water until 'al dente'. Drain, rinse and then set aside to drain well.

**2** Pound the basil leaves in a mortar and pestle, then add the garlic and pound until well mixed. Add the Parmesan and continue to pound. Transfer to a large bowl and gradually whisk in the olive oil.

**3** Melt the butter in a pan, add the pasta and place over a gentle heat. Add the basil sauce, stir well with a wooden spoon and season with salt and pepper. Serve as soon as the pasta is completely heated through.

Step 2. Pound the basil and garlic until well mixed then add the Parmesan.

Preparation takes about 25 minutes and cooking takes about 8 minutes.

Serves 4

The sauce can be made in a food processor by adding all the ingredients together and processing until smooth. This reduces the preparation time to about 3 minutes.

# Spiced Chickpeas

Preparation takes about 15 minutes, plus overnight soaking. Cooking takes about 45-50 minutes.

Serves 4

Take great care not to get the juice from the chillies into the eyes or mouth. If this happens, rinse thoroughly with cold water.

## INGREDIENTS

*460g/1lb dried chickpeas*
*1 large onion*
*2 green chillies*
*2.5cm/1-in fresh ginger*
*4 cloves garlic*
*3 tbsps oil*
*2 bay leaves*
*2.5cm/1-in cinnamon stick*
*4 black cardamom pods*
*4 green cardamom pods*
*1 tsp cumin seeds*
*4 cloves*
*1½ tsps coriander seeds*
*300ml/10 fl oz canned tomatoes*
*½ tsp salt*
*½ tsp black pepper*
*6 sprigs fresh coriander*

Step 2. Fry the bay leaves, cinnamon, ginger and garlic with the onion for 1 minute.

## METHOD

**1** Soak the chickpeas overnight in cold water. Cook the chickpeas in their soaking water until they are soft. Drain and reserve 225ml/8 fl oz of the cooking liquid.

**2** Chop the onion and slice the chillies in half lengthways, removing the seeds if a milder flavour is preferred. Grate the ginger and crush the garlic. Heat the oil in a frying pan and fry the onion gently until soft, but not coloured. Add the bay leaves, cinnamon, chillies, ginger and garlic and fry for 1 minute.

**3** Remove the seeds from both types of cardamom pods and grind in a pestle and mortar or electric coffee grinder with the cumin seeds, cloves and coriander seeds. Stir the ground spices, the tomatoes and the salt and pepper into the onions.

**4** Add the reserved chickpea cooking liquid and the drained chickpeas. Mix well. Chop the coriander leaves and sprinkle over the chickpeas. Cover and simmer for 10 minutes, adding a little extra liquid, if necessary.

# *Vegetable Ribbons with Basil Sauce*

## INGREDIENTS

*2 large courgettes*
*2 medium carrots*
*1 large or 2 small leeks*
*120g/4oz shelled*
*pistachio nuts*
*2 small shallots*
*2 tbsps chopped*
*parsley*
*90g/3oz fresh basil*
*leaves*
*280-420ml/½-¾ pt*
*olive oil*
*Salt and pepper*

## METHOD

**1** Cut the courgettes and carrots into long, thin slices with a mandolin or by hand. Cut the leeks into lengths the same size. Make sure the leeks are well rinsed in between all layers then cut into long, thin strips.

**2** Using a large, sharp knife, cut the courgette and carrot slices into long, thin strips about the thickness of 2 matchsticks.

**3** Place the carrot strips in a pan of boiling salted water and cook for about 3-4 minutes or until tender crisp. Drain and rinse under cold water. Cook the courgette strips separately for about 2-3 minutes and add the leek strips during the last 1 minute of cooking. Drain and rinse the vegetables and leave with the carrots to drain dry.

**4** Put the pistachios, roughly chopped shallots, parsley and basil in a food processor or blender and chop finely.

**5** Reserve about 3 tbsps of the olive oil for later use. With the machine running, pour the remaining oil through the funnel in a thin, steady stream. Use enough oil to bring the mixture to the consistency of mayonnaise. Add seasoning to taste.

**6** Heat reserved oil in a large pan and add the drained vegetables. Season and toss over a moderate heat until heated through. Add the sauce and toss gently to coat the vegetables. Serve immediately.

Step 2. Stack several lengths of courgette and carrot and cut into long julienne strips.

Preparation takes about 30-40 minutes and cooking takes about 10 minutes.

Serves 4

The sauce can be prepared several days in advance and kept, covered, in the refrigerator. It can also be frozen for up to 6 months.

# Celeriac à la Moutarde

Preparation takes about 10 minutes, cooking takes about 20 minutes.

Serves 4

If there are lumps in the sauce, rub it through a nylon sieve to remove them.

## INGREDIENTS

*1 large root celeriac*
*75g/2½oz butter*
*45g/1½oz plain flour*
*570ml/1 pt milk*
*60ml/4 tbsps Dijon mustard*
*1 tsp celery seeds*
*Black pepper*
*30g/4 tbsps dry breadcrumbs*

## METHOD

**1** Peel the celeriac and cut into 5mm/½-in slices and then into sticks about 2.5cm/1-in long. Cook in lightly salted boiling water for about 10 minutes or until just tender, then drain.

**2** Meanwhile melt 45g/1½ oz of the butter in a saucepan. Stir in the flour and cook for about 30 seconds. Remove from the heat and gradually add the milk, stirring well after each addition.

**3** Return to the heat and stir in the mustard, celery seeds and some freshly ground black pepper. Cook gently until thickened, stirring constantly.

**4** Add the celeriac to the sauce and stir to coat well. Transfer to a serving dish, keeping warm.

**5** Melt the remaining butter in a small frying pan and fry the breadcrumbs until golden, sprinkle the crumbs over the celeriac and serve immediately.

Step 1. Cut the celeriac into 5mm/¼-in slices and then cut each slice into 2.5cm/1-in strips.

# *Braised Fennel*

## INGREDIENTS

2 large bulbs of fennel
2 tsps chopped fresh
lovage or fennel
120ml/4 fl oz vegetable
stock
2 tbsps sherry
½ tsp celery seeds

## METHOD

**1** With a sharp knife cut away the thick root end of the fennel bulbs. Trim away the upper stalks and reserve the green feathery top for a garnish.

**2** Thickly slice the fennel, separating the strips from each other as you cut.

**3** Place the fennel, lovage, stock and sherry in a saucepan and bring gently to the boil. Reduce the heat and simmer gently for about 15 minutes or until fennel is tender.

**4** Drain and transfer to a warm serving dish. Sprinkle with celery seeds and garnish with the fennel fronds.

Step 1. Using a sharp knife, trim away any thick root from the fennel bulbs.

Preparation takes about 10 minutes, cooking takes about 15 minutes.

Serves 4

For a delicious variation add 1 peeled, cored and thinly sliced cooking apple to the fennel.

# *Herb Rice Pilaff*

Preparation takes about 20 minutes and cooking takes about 20-25 minutes.

Serves 6

The rice must simmer very slowly if it is to absorb all the water without overcooking. Add extra water or pour some off as necessary during cooking, depending on how much liquid the rice has absorbed.

## INGREDIENTS

2 tbsps oil
30g/1oz butter
175g/6oz long-grain rice
570ml/1 pt boiling water
Salt and pepper
90g/3oz mixed fresh herbs (parsley, thyme, marjoram, basil)
1 small bunch spring onions

## METHOD

**1** Heat the oil in a large, heavy-based saucepan and add the butter. When foaming, add the rice and cook over a moderate heat for about 2 minutes, stirring constantly.

**2** When the rice begins to look opaque, add the water, salt and pepper and bring to the boil, stirring occasionally.

**3** Cover the pan and reduce the heat. Simmer very gently, without stirring, for about 20 minutes or until all the liquid has been absorbed and the rice is tender.

**4** Chop the herbs and spring onions very finely and stir into the rice. Cover the pan and leave to stand for about 5 minutes before serving.

Step 1. Cook the rice in the oil and butter until it begins to turn opaque.

Step 4. Stir the onions and herbs into the rice and fluff up the grains with a fork.

# Spaghetti Rice

## INGREDIENTS

*120g/4oz spaghetti*
*120g/4oz long-grain rice*
*3 tbsps oil*
*4 tbsps sesame seeds*
*2 tbsps chopped chives*
*Salt and pepper*
*420ml/¾ pt stock*
*1 tbsp soy sauce*
*2 tbsps chopped parsley*

## METHOD

1. Break the spaghetti into 5cm/2-in pieces and rinse with the rice under running water. Leave to drain dry.

2. Heat the oil in a large frying pan and add the dried rice and pasta. Cook over a moderate heat to brown the rice and pasta, stirring continuously.

3. Add the sesame seeds and cook until the rice, pasta and seeds are golden brown.

4. Add the chives, salt and pepper, and pour over 280ml/½ pint of the stock. Stir in the soy sauce and bring to the boil.

5. Cover and cook about 20 minutes, or until the rice and pasta are tender and the stock is absorbed. Add more of the reserved stock as necessary. Do not let the rice and pasta dry out during cooking.

6. Fluff up the grains of rice with a fork and sprinkle with the parsley before serving.

Step 2. Cook the rice and pasta in the oil until just beginning to brown.

Step 5. Cook until all the liquid is absorbed and the pasta and rice are tender.

Preparation takes about 25 minutes and cooking takes about 20 minutes.

Serves 4

Serve as a side dish with meat or poultry. Give it an Italian flavour by omitting sesame seeds, chives and soy sauce. Substitute Parmesan and basil instead.

# Poached Pears with Raspberry Coulis

Preparation takes about 20 minutes, plus chilling. Cooking takes about 10 minutes.

Serves 4

The raspberries can be puréed by simply rubbing through a sieve but blending in a food processor or liquidiser first makes the job much easier.

INGREDIENTS

*280ml/½ pt water*
*60ml/4 tbsps clear honey*
*1 tbsp lemon juice*
*2 sprigs fresh hyssop*
*4 pears*
*225g/8oz raspberries*
*1 tsp chopped fresh hyssop*
***Decoration:***
*Sprigs of fresh hyssop*

METHOD

**1** Place the water and honey in a large saucepan or frying pan and heat until the honey dissolves. Stir in the lemon juice and hyssop sprigs.

**2** Peel the pears and carefully cut them in half lengthways using a sharp knife. Keeping the stalks intact if possible, remove the core with a grapefruit knife or teaspoon.

**3** Put the pears in the syrup and bring gently to the boil. Cover, reduce the heat and simmer gently for 5 minutes or until the pears are tender. The exact cooking time will depend on the type and size of the pears and the degree of ripeness. Chill until required.

**4** Meanwhile, purée the raspberries and chopped hyssop in a food processor or liquidiser and push through a sieve to remove the seeds. Sweeten the raspberry coulis with a little of the honey syrup if wished.

**5** Arrange the pears on a serving plate and pour a little of the raspberry coulis over each. Decorate with sprigs of hyssop and serve the remaining sauce separately.

Step 2. Keeping the stalks intact, carefully remove the cores from the pears using a grapefruit knife.

# Spiced Crème Brûlée

## INGREDIENTS

280ml/½ pt milk
1 stick cinnamon
2 tbsps coriander seeds
1 vanilla pod
4 egg yolks
1½ tbsps cornflour
90g/3oz caster sugar
280ml/½ pt double cream
60ml/4 tbsps brown sugar

## METHOD

1 Put the milk into a pan and add the cinnamon, coriander and vanilla pod. Heat gently until beginning to boil. Cool completely.

2 In a bowl, whisk the egg yolks, cornflour and caster sugar until thick and creamy.

3 Strain the milk through a sieve. Put into a pan along with the cream, and heat until just below boiling. Beat into the egg yolk mixture, pouring gradually and whisking constantly until smooth.

4 Rinse out the pan and return the custard to it. Cook over a very gentle heat until almost boiling, stirring all the time with a wooden spoon until the mixture is thick enough to coat the back of it. Do not allow to boil. Divide the custard between 4 ramekins. Chill until set.

5 Stand the ramekins in a roasting tin and surround them with ice. Preheat a grill to its highest temperature. Sprinkle the sugar evenly over the custards and put under the grill. Turn frequently and move the tin around until the sugar melts and caramelises. Chill until the sugar is hard and crisp.

Step 2. When lifted, the mixture should leave a trail on its surface.

Step 4. Cook the custard until thick enough to coat a wooden spoon.

Preparation takes 15 minutes, cooking takes 30 minutes.

Serves 4

Do not boil either the milk and cream mixture or the egg yolk mixture, as this will result in curdling and the custard will not be smooth.

# *Applemint Pudding*

Preparation takes about 20 minutes and cooking takes 2-2½ hours.

Serves 4-6

Serve with cream or ice cream.

## INGREDIENTS

225g/8oz cooking apples
Nut of butter
30g/1oz caster sugar
120g/4oz soft brown sugar
1 tbsp chopped fresh applemint
120g/4oz butter
2 eggs, beaten
120g/4oz self-raising flour
3 tbsps milk

## METHOD

**1** Peel, core and slice the apples. Place in a small saucepan with the nut of butter and caster sugar and cook gently until they form a thick purée.

**2** Stir 1 tbsp of the applemint into the cooked apples, allow to cool then spoon into the bottom of a well greased 1.1ltr/2 pt pudding basin.

**3** Place the butter in a mixing bowl and beat lightly to soften. Add the soft brown sugar and beat until pale and creamy. Gradually add the eggs, beating well after each addition. Fold in the flour, remaining applemint and the milk, using a metal tablespoon, to make a cake batter of a soft dropping consistency.

**4** Spoon the cake mixture over the apple purée in the pudding basin, smoothing the top. Cover with a piece of greased, pleated greasproof paper and foil then secure with string. Steam in a double boiler or place in a large saucepan and pour enough boiling water around the basin to come half way up the sides. Cover the pan tightly and leave to steam for 2-2½ hours, topping up the water level with more boiling water if necessary.

**5** Remove the foil and greaseproof paper from the top of the pudding. Invert a serving plate over the top of the basin and carefully turn both over, gently shaking the basin to ease the pudding out onto the plate.

Step 3. Fold the remaining applemint into the cake mixture.

# *Chocolate Spice Cake*

## INGREDIENTS

*5 eggs, separated*
*175g/6oz caster sugar*
*90g/3oz plain*
*chocolate, melted*
*90g/3oz plain flour*
*½ tsp ground nutmeg*
*½ tsp ground cinnamon*
*½ tsp ground cloves*
***Topping:***
*1 tbsp icing sugar*
*1 tsp ground cinnamon*

Step 2. Whisk the egg yolks and sugar together vigorously until they are as thick and creamy as softly whipped double cream.

Step 6. Mix together the icing sugar and cinnamon and sieve this over the cake.

## METHOD

**1** Grease and line a 20cm/8-inch spring-form cake tin with greasproof paper. Brush the paper with melted butter and dust with a little flour.

**2** Put the egg yolks and sugar into a mixing bowl and whisk them hard, until the mixture is thick, pale and creamy. Stir in the melted chocolate. Sift the flour and spices over, then carefully fold in with a metal tablespoon.

**3** Whisk the egg whites until they form soft peaks. Fold these carefully into the chocolate mixture.

**4** Gently pour the cake mixture into the prepared tin and bake in an oven preheated to 180°C/350°F/Gas Mark 4, for 40-45 minutes, or until a skewer inserted into the middle of the cake comes out clean.

**5** Leave the cake to cool in the tin for 10 minutes, then turn out onto a wire rack and leave to cool completely.

**6** Mix together the icing sugar and cinnamon. Sieve this over the top of the cake, before serving.

Preparation takes 30 minutes and cooking takes 40-45 minutes.

Makes 1x20cm/8-in cake.

Decorate the cake with whipped cream and serve with fresh strawberries.

# *Rice Pudding*

Preparation takes 10 minutes and cooking takes about 1¼ hours.

Serves 4

Frequent stirring is important in this recipe to prevent the pudding from burning and giving a bitter flavour to the dessert.

### INGREDIENTS
175g/6oz pudding rice
60g/2oz unsalted butter
1 bay leaf
2.5cm/1-in cinnamon stick
1.2 ltrs/2 pts milk
175g/6oz granulated sugar
400ml/⅔ pt evaporated milk
8 green cardamoms
60g/2oz chopped blanched almonds
30g/1oz shelled pistachio nuts

### METHOD

❶ Wash the rice under running water then leave to drain thoroughly. Melt the butter in a saucepan and fry the bay leaf and cinnamon for 1 minute. Add the rice and stir well to coat evenly with the butter.

❷ Add the milk and bring the mixture to the boil, then reduce the heat and simmer for 40-50 minutes, stirring occasionally to prevent the rice from sticking to the pan.

❸ Add the sugar and the evaporated milk to the rice mixture and continue cooking for a further 20-30 minutes, stirring frequently to prevent burning. It is important to keep stirring the mixture during this cooking time to bring up thin layers of light brown skin which form on the base of the saucepan. This is what gives the pudding its rich, reddish tinge and caramel flavour.

❹ Remove the seeds from the cardamoms and crush them. Discard the bay leaf and cinnamon from the rice and add the almonds and crushed cardamoms. Stir the pudding well and pour into a large serving dish. Decorate the top of the pudding with slivered pistachio nuts, and serve hot or cold.

Step 3. Stir the pudding frequently to bring up the thin layers of light brown skin which will form on the base of the saucepan during cooking.

# *Spiced Oranges with Honey and Mint*

*280ml/½ pt clear honey*
*420ml/¾ pt water*
*2 large sprigs of fresh mint*
*12 whole cloves*
*4 large oranges*
**Decoration:**
*4 small sprigs of mint*

METHOD

**1** Put the honey and the water into a heavy-based saucepan. Add the mint and cloves, and slowly bring to the boil. Stir the mixture to dissolve the honey and boil rapidly for 5 minutes, or until the liquid is very syrupy.

**2** Cool the mixture completely, then strain the syrup through a nylon sieve into a jug or bowl to remove the mint and cloves.

**3** Using a potato peeler, carefully pare the rind very thinly from one orange. Cut the pared orange rind into very fine julienne shreds with a sharp knife.

**4** Put the shreds of orange peel into a small bowl and cover with boiling water. Allow to stand until cold then drain completely. Stir the strips of peel into the honey syrup and chill well.

**5** Peel the oranges completely, cutting off all the white pith. Slice the oranges into thin rounds using a sharp knife. Arrange the orange rounds on four individual serving plates.

**6** Pour the chilled syrup over the oranges on the plates and decorate with the small sprigs of mint just before serving.

Step 2. Strain the syrup through a nylon sieve into a jug or bowl to remove the sprigs of mint and cloves.

Step 3. Carefully pare the rind from one of the oranges, using a potato peeler and making sure that no white pith comes away with the rind.

Preparation takes 20 minutes and cooking takes about 5 minutes.

Serves 4

It is important that all the white pith is removed from the oranges, otherwise this will give a bitter flavour to the dessert.

# *Baked Carrot Custard*

Preparation takes about 15 minutes, cooking takes about 40-50 minutes.

Serves 4

If you have a food processor, you can save time by using the grating attachment to prepare the carrots.

### INGREDIENTS

*460g/1lb carrots*
*140ml/¼ pt water*
*120g/4oz pitted dates*
*1 tsp ground cinnamon*
*½ tsp ground nutmeg*
*¼ tsp ground ginger*
*¼ tsp ground cloves*
*3 eggs (size 2), beaten*
*60g/2oz pistachio nuts*
*420ml/¾ pt milk*
***Decoration:***
*Pistachio nuts*

### METHOD

❶ Using the coarse side of a grater, grate the carrots. Place in a saucepan, add the water and simmer gently for 5 minutes or until soft.

❷ Finely chop the dates, add to the pan and cook for a further 3 minutes.

❸ Place the carrot mixture into a food processor or liquidiser and process to make a fine purée.

❹ Transfer to a large mixing bowl. Stir in the spices, then beat in the eggs. Chop the pistachios and add to the bowl.

❺ Heat the milk until almost boiling, then beat into the carrot mixture. Transfer to a shallow ovenproof serving dish and bake in an oven preheated to 160°C/325°F/Gas Mark 3 for 40-45 minutes or until set.

❻ Allow the custard to cool slightly and serve warm, or chill completely before serving. Decorate with extra pistachio nuts.

Step 5. Cook the custard until the centre is just set and the outer edges are firm.

# *Thyme Sorbet*

INGREDIENTS

*520ml/18 fl oz water*
*150g/5oz sugar*
*4 small sprigs fresh*
*thyme in flower*

METHOD

**1** Boil together the water and sugar until a reasonably thick syrup is formed – this will take about 15 minutes boiling.

**2** Remove from the heat and add the sprigs of thyme. Remove the thyme from the syrup after 2 minutes and drain the syrup through a very fine sieve.

**3** Pour the syrup into an ice cream maker and set in motion.*

**4** When the sorbet has crystallized spoon into a container and keep in the freezer until needed.

*If an ice cream maker is not available, pour the strained syrup into a shallow container and place in the freezer until partially frozen. Remove from freezer, gently break the mixture up with a fork, then return to the freezer and freeze overnight before using.

Preparation takes about 30 minutes and crystallizing the sorbet takes about ¹/₂-1 hour in an ice cream maker. If using the freezer method allow at least 6 hours for the sorbet to freeze, and leave overnight.

Serves 4

Do not allow the thyme to remain in the syrup for longer than 2 minutes; the flavour is transferred very quickly.

Step 2. Drain the syrup through a very fine sieve.

#  Index